Word Hunt 2

Words! Words! Everywhere! Learn to Spell with a Scavenger Hunt for Active Kids!

30 Fun Games

Look for words all over the place! And discover how to read and spell!

The Thinking Tree

The Thinking TREE

www.DyslexiaGames.com

**Dyslexia Games
Friendly Copyright Notice:**

The Thinking Tree LLC   ●   617 N Swope St.   ●   Greenfield, IN 46140   ●   info@dyslexiagames.com   ●   +1 317-622-8852

Word Hunt 2

Words! Words! Everywhere! Learn to Spell with a Scavenger Hunt for Active Kids!

By Sarah J. Brown & Anna Brown

Parent Teacher Instructions:

Provide the student with a sharp pencil, eraser, a set of sharp colored pencils, if he wants to color in the pictures.

This is a game of discovery for active children who enjoy exploring their world.

Show your child how to go on a scavenger hunt for words with three to eight letters. Each time the child finds a word with the right number of letters he will write it down on the page. The child is learning to recognize words, become familiar with the spelling of many words, and is beginning to learn the structure of the words in his own world. Since this game is fun for kids they will be more likely to remember how to spell the words that they discover.

Additional games and activities are found on many pages to keep the creative area of the mind engaged in the writing process.

For best results:
Reward your child with a prize for completing each page!

If your child has shown improvement but is still reversing any letters in this exercise, continue with Series B –Book 1.

Find 20 THREE Letter Words

jam

Look all around your house for 3 letter words.
TIP: Look in books, on boxes, and on food labels.

Name:_____   Date:_____

Find 20
THREE Letter Words

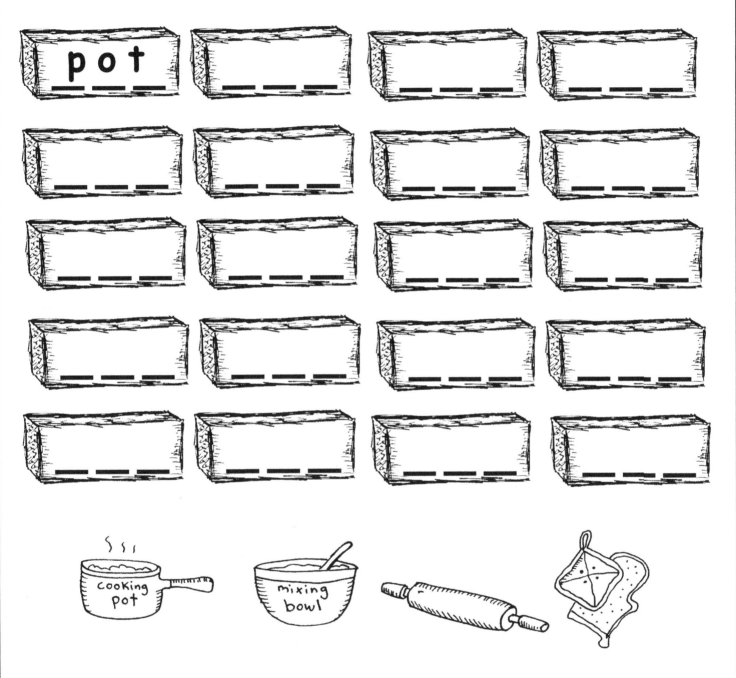

Look all around your house for 3 letter words.
TIP: Look in books, on boxes, and on food labels.

Name:_____ Date:_____

Find 20
THREE Letter Words

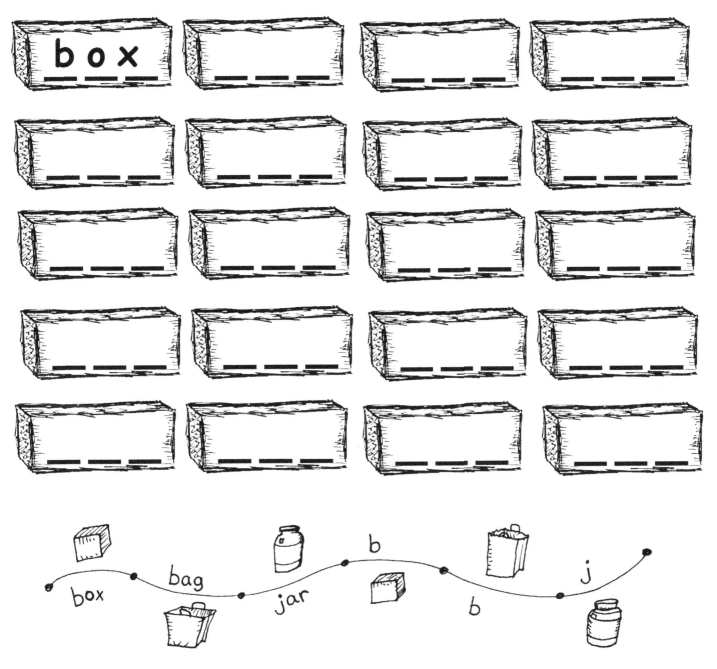

b o x

Look all around your house for 3 letter words.
TIP: Look in books, on boxes, and on food labels.

Name:_____   Date:_____

Find 20
THREE Letter Words

car

Look all around your house for 3 letter words.
TIP: Look in books, on boxes, and on food labels.

Name:_____   Date:_____

Find 20 FOUR Letter Words

milk

Look all around your house for 4 letter words.
TIP: Look in books, on boxes, and on food labels.

Name:_____ Date:_____

Find 20
FOUR Letter Words

s o u p

Look all around your house for 4 letter words.
TIP: Look in books, on boxes, and on food labels.

Name:_____   Date:_____

Find 20
FOUR Letter Words

cook

Look all around your house for 4 letter words.
TIP: Look in books, on boxes, and on food labels.

Name:_____ Date:_____

Find 20 FOUR Letter Words

s a l t

Look all around your house for 4 letter words.
TIP: Look in books, on boxes, and on food labels.

Name:_____ Date:_____

Find 15
FIVE Letter Words

cloud

Look all around your house for 5 letter words.
TIP: Look in books, on boxes, and on food labels.

Name:_____   **Date:**_____

Find 15 FIVE Letter Words

house

Look all around your house for 5 letter words.
TIP: Look in books, on boxes, and on food labels.

Name:_____   Date:_____

Find 15
FIVE Letter Words

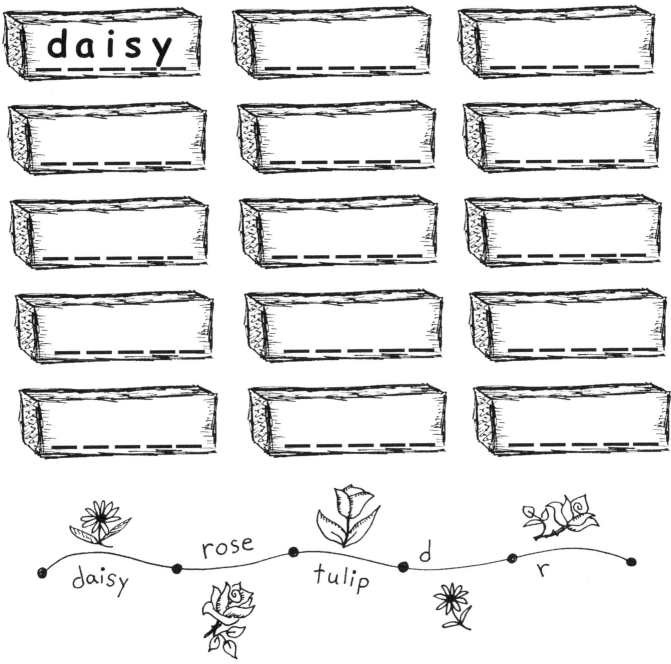

daisy

rose

tulip

daisy

d

r

Look all around your house for 5 letter words.
TIP: Look in books, on boxes, and on food labels.

Name:_____ Date:_____

Find 15 FIVE Letter Words

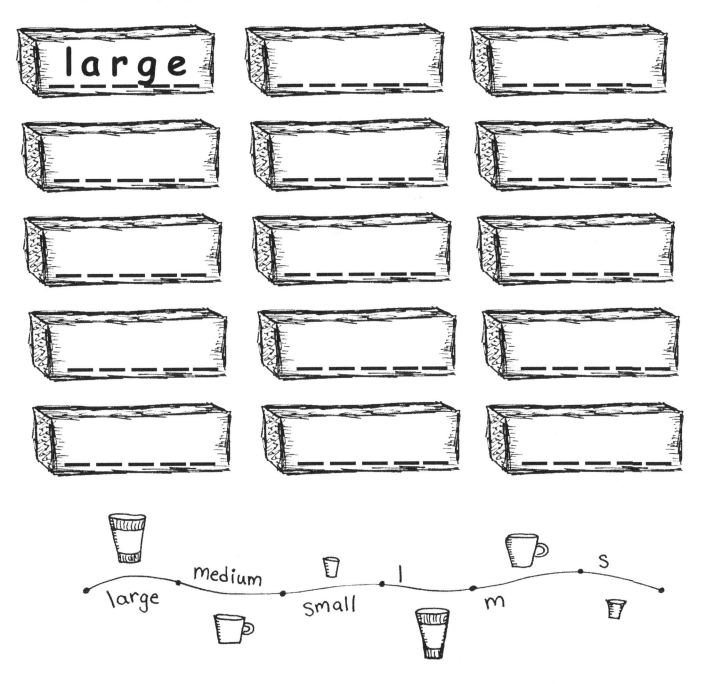

large

Look all around your house for 5 letter words.
TIP: Look in books, on boxes, and on food labels.

Name:_____ Date:_____

Find 15 FIVE Letter Words

house

Look all around your house for 5 letter words.
TIP: Look in books, on boxes, and on food labels.

Name:_____ Date:_____

Find 15
SIX Letter Words

cherry

Look all around your house for 6 letter words.
TIP: Look in books, on boxes, and on food labels.

Name:_____ Date:_____

Find 15
SIX Letter Words

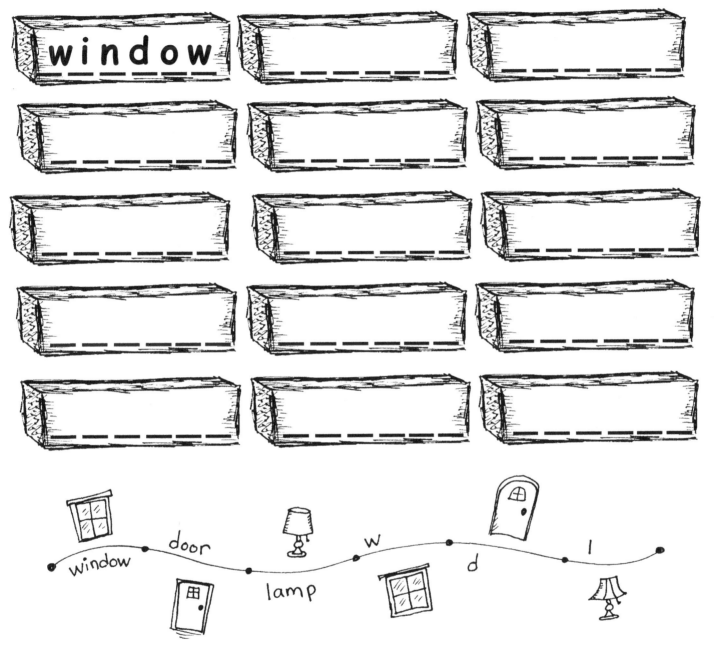

w i n d o w

Look all around your house for 6 letter words.
TIP: Look in books, on boxes, and on food labels.

Name:_____   Date:_____

Find 15
SIX Letter Words

donkey

Look all around your house for 6 letter words.
TIP: Look in books, on boxes, and on food labels.

Name:_____ Date:_____

Find 15
SIX Letter Words

cookie

Look all around your house for 6 letter words.
TIP: Look in books, on boxes, and on food labels.

Name:_____ Date:_____

Find 15 SIX Letter Words

turtle

Look all around your house for 6 letter words.
TIP: Look in books, on boxes, and on food labels.

Name:_____ Date:_____

Find 15
SIX Letter Words

pizzas

Look all around your house for 6 letter words.
TIP: Look in books, on boxes, and on food labels.

Name:_____ Date:_____

Find 10 SEVEN Letter Words

rooster

snail

Rooster
rooster

Turtle
turtle

Goat
goat

Hamster
hamster

Look all around your house for 7 letter words.
TIP: Look in books, on boxes, and on food labels.

Name:_____   Date:_____

Find 10
SEVEN Letter Words

cookies

Look all around your house for 7 letter words.
TIP: Look in books, on boxes, and on food labels.

Name:_____   Date:_____

Find 10
SEVEN Letter Words

kittens

Look all around your house for 7 letter words.
TIP: Look in books, on boxes, and on food labels.

Name:_____ Date:_____

Find 10
SEVEN Letter Words

carrots

Look all around your house for 7 letter words.
TIP: Look in books, on boxes, and on food labels.

Name:_____ Date:_____

Find 10 EIGHT Letter Words

duckling

Look all around your house for 8 letter words.
TIP: Look in books, on boxes, and on food labels.

Name:_____ Date:_____

Find 10 EIGHT Letter Words

Dinosaur

Look all around your house for 8 letter words.
TIP: Look in books, on boxes, and on food labels.

Name:_____ Date:_____

Find 10 EIGHT Letter Words

Umbrella

pears 25¢

Lemons 15¢

potatoes 20¢ each

Look all around your house for 8 letter words.
TIP: Look in books, on boxes, and on food labels

Name:_____ Date:_____

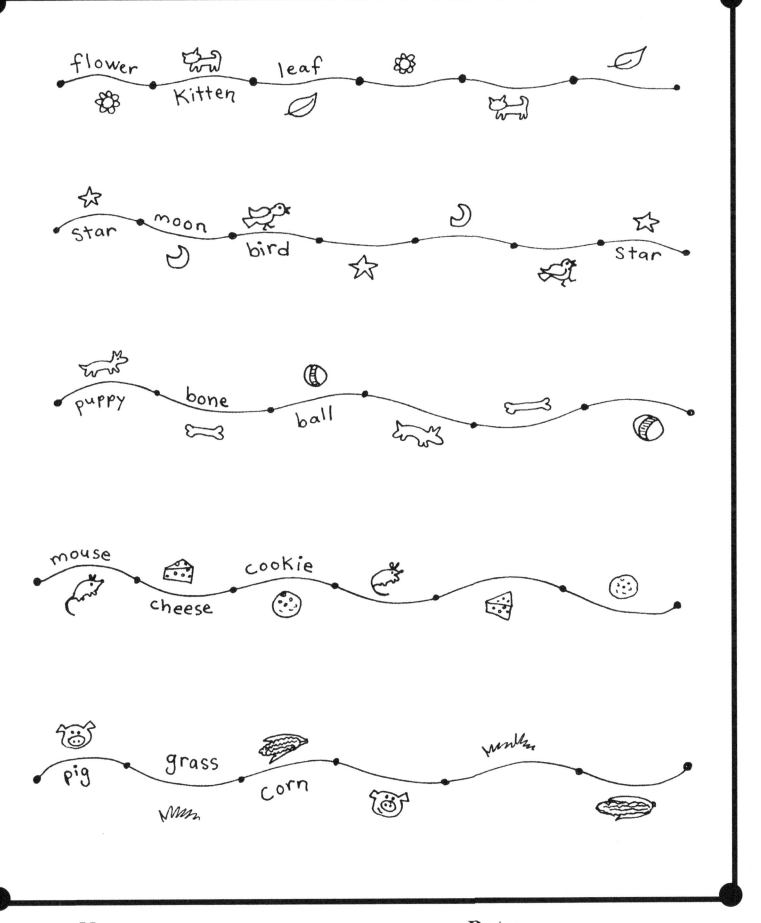

flower · · leaf · · ·
· Kitten · · cat

star · moon · bird · · · · star

puppy · bone · · ball · · ·

mouse · cheese · cookie · · · ·

pig · grass · corn · · · ·

Name:_____ **Date:**_____

Name:_____ Date:_____

WORD HUNT

Certificate of Completion

_____

Name & Age

_____

Date of Completion

The Thinking
TREE

_____

Dyslexia Games

_____

Teacher

DyslexiaGames.com

Word Hunt
Discover the Words in Your World!

Find 4
SIX Letter Words

turtle

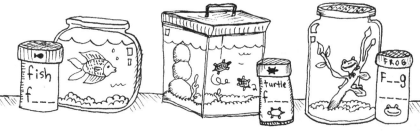

Look all around your house
for 6 letter words.
TIP: Look in books,
on boxes, and on food labels

30 GAMES

"Finally, a fun solution for reading confusion!"

 DyslexiaGames.com

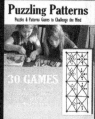

Made in the USA
Middletown, DE
09 April 2021